COUNTERING TRUTH DECAY A RAND Initiative to Restore the Role of Facts and Analysis in Public Life

ENGAGING YOUTH WITH
PUBLIC POLICY

Middle School Lessons to Counter Truth Decay

Andrea Prado Tuma   Alice Huguet

Sponsored by Zwick Impact Fund

For more information on this publication, visit **www.rand.org/t/TLA387-1**.

About RAND

The RAND Corporation is a research organization that develops solutions to public policy challenges to help make communities throughout the world safer and more secure, healthier and more prosperous. RAND is nonprofit, nonpartisan, and committed to the public interest. To learn more about RAND, visit www.rand.org.

Research Integrity

Our mission to help improve policy and decisionmaking through research and analysis is enabled through our core values of quality and objectivity and our unwavering commitment to the highest level of integrity and ethical behavior. To help ensure our research and analysis are rigorous, objective, and nonpartisan, we subject our research publications to a robust and exacting quality-assurance process; avoid both the appearance and reality of financial and other conflicts of interest through staff training, project screening, and a policy of mandatory disclosure; and pursue transparency in our research engagements through our commitment to the open publication of our research findings and recommendations, disclosure of the source of funding of published research, and policies to ensure intellectual independence. For more information, visit www.rand.org/about/research-integrity.

RAND's publications do not necessarily reflect the opinions of its research clients and sponsors.

Published by the RAND Corporation, Santa Monica, Calif.
© 2022 RAND Corporation
RAND® is a registered trademark.

Library of Congress Cataloging-in-Publication Data is available for this publication.
ISBN: 978-1-9774-0943-0

Cover and interior design: Rick Penn-Kraus

Photo credits:

Cover:
 Top: SDI Productions/Getty Images
 Bottom left: dusanpetkovic/Getty Images/iStockphoto
 Bottom right: Creatas Images/Getty Images
 Capitol: Rick Penn-Kraus
Page iv: fstop123/Getty Images
Page 2: kali9/Getty Images
Page 5: diego_cervo/Getty Images/iStockphoto
Page 8: SDI Productions/Getty Images
Page 9: aldomurillo/Getty Images/iStockphoto
Page 10: michaeljung/Getty Images/iStockphoto
Page 14: SDI Productions/Getty Images/iStockphoto
Page 18: fotosipsak/Getty Images
Page 22: RichLegg/Getty Images
Page 26: SDI Productions/Getty Images
Page 31: PeopleImages/Getty Images/iStockphoto
Page 32: Fly View Productions/Getty Images

Contents

About This Tool

This educational tool is part of the Countering Truth Decay initiative, which is focused on restoring the role of facts, data, and analysis in U.S. political and civil discourse and the policymaking process. The phrase *Truth Decay* refers to the diminishing role of facts, data, and analysis in our political and civic lives that has stymied public discourse (Kavanagh and Rich, 2018). The consequences of Truth Decay are dire—including political paralysis and individual alienation from civic life—and require attention. At the RAND Corporation, we are exploring education as one approach to countering Truth Decay. With this imperative in mind, we developed an educational tool, consisting of five sequenced lesson plans for middle school teachers, that aims to engage youth with RAND policy research. Our goal is to improve RAND's outreach to this audience in ways that also help counter Truth Decay. The lesson plans will help students understand the following:

- how public policy relates to their own lives
- why it is important to learn about public policy topics from credible sources
- how to be more critical consumers and creators of information.

The lessons culminate with students applying what they learn about a public policy topic—via a question-and-answer (Q&A) video with a RAND expert, a student-friendly Q&A document, and their own investigation into the topic—to create an information product that can be used to communicate policy-relevant concepts to their peers. In the introduction, we discuss the motivation for the lesson plans, provide information about how to implement the lessons, and explain some of the ways they can be modified to fit varying student needs and contexts.

More information about RAND can be found at www.rand.org. Questions about this tool should be directed to apradotu@rand.org.

Countering Truth Decay

This educational tool is part of the Countering Truth Decay initiative. The original report, *Truth Decay: An Initial Exploration of the Diminishing Role of Facts and Analysis in American Public Life*, by Jennifer Kavanagh and Michael D. Rich, was published in January 2018 and identified a research agenda for studying and developing solutions to the Truth Decay challenge. In July of the following year, the RAND Corporation released a follow-up report linking media literacy to Truth Decay (Huguet, Kavanagh, et al., 2019). That was followed by several reports in 2020 and 2021:

- Laura S. Hamilton, Julia H. Kaufman, and Lynn Hu, *Media Use and Literacy in Schools: Civic Development in the Era of Truth Decay*, RR-A112-2, 2020a
- Laura S. Hamilton, Julia H. Kaufman, and Lynn Hu, *Preparing Children and Youth for Civic Life in the Era of Truth Decay: Insights from the American Teacher Panel*, RR-A112-6, 2020b
- Alice Huguet, Garrett Baker, Laura S. Hamilton, and John F. Pane, *Media*

Literacy Standards to Counter Truth Decay, RR-A112-12, 2021

- Alice Huguet, John F. Pane, Garrett Baker, Laura S. Hamilton, and Susannah Faxon-Mills, *Media Literacy Education to Counter Truth Decay: An Implementation and Evaluation Framework*, RR-A112-18, 2021.

This educational tool builds on RAND's work on Truth Decay and provides middle school teachers with sequenced lesson plans that aim to engage youth with policy research in ways that also help counter Truth Decay.

Funding

The development and publication of this tool was made possible by a gift from the late Charles J. Zwick and his wife, Barbara. In 2011, Zwick, a RAND researcher and former trustee, established a $1 million charitable fund to help meet RAND's most pressing research needs. Zwick Impact Awards extend works on completed research projects to extend their visibility and reach, helping to move them closer to having impact and making a difference to communities throughout the world.

Acknowledgments

We would like to acknowledge the educators and students at the Boys & Girls Club of Dorchester and Belvedere Middle School, who played an invaluable role in the development of this tool. Their time and willingness to collaborate with us on piloting these lesson plans were immensely helpful for this effort and for helping us understand more about how to engage youth with public policy topics. In addition, we thank the researchers who participated in the pilot workshops: Matthew Mizel, Mahshid Abir, Julia Kaufman, and Jhacova Williams.

We are also extremely grateful to the researchers—Mahshid Abir, Shelly Culbertson, Robert Lempert, and Wendy Troxel—who worked with us to create informational documents and videos for middle school students about policy-relevant topics. We are equally grateful to the students—Elisabeth, Kyra, Colette, and Alana—who participated in the videos, and we thank their parents for their help with coordination and technical support. We also extend a sincere thanks to our quality assurance manager, Katherine Carman, and to reviewers Elaine Wang and Tessa Jolls, who provided constructive feedback that improved the lesson plans. We are also grateful to Jennifer McCombs for her feedback on this project, Katheryn Giglio, who provided expert editing to help us create student-friendly documents, Arwen Bicknell for her editing of the tool, and Marissa Norris for her project management assistance. We also appreciate the efforts of the RAND multimedia team, especially Emily Ashenfelter, for the work that went into video production and editing.

About the Lesson Plans

In this tool, we outline five sequenced lesson plans for middle school teachers. The overarching goals of the lessons are to help students understand the following:

- how public policy relates to their own lives
- why it is important to learn about public policy topics (such as climate change, coronavirus disease 2019 [COVID-19], immigration, and school start times and their impact on sleep) from credible sources
- how to be more-critical consumers and creators of information.

The five lessons align with Common Core State Standards (CCSS) for English Language Arts/Literacy for grades 6 through 8 (Common Core State Standards Initiative, 2010); they also contain connections to RAND's Truth Decay Media Literacy Standards (Huguet, Baker, et al., 2021). Additionally, we provide connections to the P21 Framework for 21st Century Learning Competencies (Battelle for Kids, undated) and one Next Generation Science Standard (Next Generation Science Standards, undated). (For more details, see Appendix B). The lesson plans culminate with students applying what they learn about a public policy topic—via a question-and-answer (Q&A) video with a RAND expert, a student-friendly Q&A document, and their own investigation into the topic—to create an information product that can be used to communicate policy-relevant concepts to their peers. In this introduction, we discuss the motivation for the lesson plans, provide information about how to implement the lessons, and explain some of the ways they can be modified to fit student needs and contexts.

Motivation for the Lessons

The primary motivation behind these lessons is to counter the continued spread of Truth Decay. We use the phrase Truth Decay as shorthand for the diminishing role of facts, data, and analysis in our political and civic lives that has stymied public discourse (Kavanagh and Rich, 2018). The consequences of Truth Decay are dire—including political paralysis and individual alienation from civic life—and require attention. At the RAND Corporation, we are exploring education as a crucial approach to countering Truth Decay. Kindergarten through 12th-grade (K–12) school systems have a wide reach and are an important venue for students' development as participating members of society. We suggest greater instruction related to civic education (including exposing students to public policy issues) and media literacy (ML) education, two topics that inform these lessons.

Why Teach Students About Public Policy?

Education plays a key role not only in preparing students to succeed in college and their professional lives but also in preparing them to become informed citizens who contribute to their community and country. Civic education can be a particularly useful tool in countering Truth Decay and growing distrust in democratic institutions (Hamilton, Kaufman, and Hu, 2020b; Levine and Kawashima-Ginsberg, 2017). Specifically, an ability to identify misinformation about public policy topics may be essential as students learn to become active participants in our democracy

(Hamilton, Kaufman, and Hu, 2020b). Furthermore, a growing body of research shows that civic education can influence long-term outcomes, such as voting and volunteering in adulthood, and can have a positive impact on career readiness (e.g., Hart et al., 2007; Kawashima-Ginsberg and Levine, 2014; Levine and Kawashima-Ginsberg, 2017). Although 39 states require at least one course in American government or civics, a 2020 RAND survey of a nationally representative sample of social studies teachers shows that many educators support civic education but do not feel prepared to teach it (Hamilton, Kaufman, and Hu, 2020b). Given the importance of civic education and interest from educators in this topic, these lesson plans can help teachers introduce middle school students to a key element of civic education: understanding and engaging with public policy topics.

> **Civic education:** the process through which schools and other institutions can help students develop civic knowledge, skills, and dispositions that will prepare them to engage in civic life (Hamilton, Kaufman, and Hu, 2020b).

Public policy directly and indirectly affects many aspects of students' lives and those of their families, such as access to health care, working conditions, and access to educational opportunities. Therefore, understanding what public policy is and how citizens can play a role in policy decisions is a critical concept for students to explore at a young age. Furthermore, because public policy addresses wide-ranging challenges facing society, we can introduce the topic of public policy as it relates to real-world issues that students might already care about. Our lesson plans aim to build students' understanding of and engagement with public policy by incorporating concepts and activities that will allow students to understand how public policy topics are relevant to their lives and how public policy can help address some of the most pressing challenges that our society faces today.

Why Integrate Components of Media Literacy?

Truth Decay has been brought on, at least in part, by an evolving information ecosystem. Understanding how to navigate our oversaturated media landscape is key not only to students' individual success, but to the health of our democracy (Jolls and Johnsen, 2018; Tully and Vraga, 2018). ML education is one particularly promising tool to counter Truth Decay. The term *media literacy* is defined differently depending on the source; overall the concept focuses on teaching students to critically interact with media in all forms, both as consumers and creators of information. A central concept in ML is that all media are constructed for a purpose and inherently contain some degree of bias or filter.

Recent research shows that large majorities of students lack the knowledge and skills needed to interpret media accurately. For example, two-thirds of middle school students in a recent study could not differentiate between news stories and ads on a website (Breakstone et al., 2019), and it is unclear whether students exit K-12 education systems any better equipped to discern between real and "fake" news (Leeder, 2019). The danger of this is that students are susceptible to misinformation, disinformation, and bias, and therefore could take misinformed stances on matters big and small; these consequences can become increasingly serious as students mature and assume a more influential role in civic life (e.g., voting).

> **Media literacy** education provides a framework to access, analyze, evaluate, create, and participate with media messages in a variety of forms — from print to video to the Internet (Center for Media Literacy, 2005).

Most teachers believe that it is important for their students to learn skills related to ML (Hamilton, Kaufman, and Hu, 2020b), but haphazard availability of resources and limited or nonexistent teacher training can make it difficult to know where to start. In a 2020 RAND American Educator Panels (AEP) survey, more than 50 percent of teachers agreed that the following were obstacles to promoting ML instruction at their schools: a lack of instructional resources, a lack of guidance about ML programs and curricula, and a lack of guidance about how to integrate ML with their classes (Baker et al., 2021). These surveys highlighted the need for a learning agenda that supports teachers in developing their ML knowledge and skills, and we recommend developing such an agenda, although doing so was beyond the scope of this project. Relatedly, researchers have identified ML as a key strategy in promoting students' civic development (Hamilton, Kaufman, and Hu, 2020b).

Studies have also found inequities in student access to ML content. For instance, a recent survey found that teachers serving majority-Black student populations were significantly less likely than those serving at majority-White schools to integrate ML concepts into their core instruction (Baker et al., 2021). Disparities like these are borne out in student competencies, as well. Black and Latinx students score below their White and Asian peers in distinguishing news from advertising, and students eligible for free or reduced-price lunch (FRPL), a rough indicator of family income, had lower scores than those *not* eligible for FRPL (Breakstone et al., 2019). These statistics underscore the urgency of equitably providing ML opportunities for all students.

With this imperative in mind, each lesson in this sequence incorporates ML competencies relevant to countering Truth Decay. We cover the following competencies (which are not inclusive of all ML knowledge and skills):

- Recognize limitations of one's own knowledge or understanding of the facts.

- Identify the expertise (e.g., academic credential, office held, firsthand knowledge) and consider the motivations (e.g., political, financial) of the creator of an information product.

- Anticipate and monitor intended and unintended consequences of what is shared in digital spaces.

- Take action rooted in evidence (e.g., construct new knowledge, create and share media, engage in informed conversations and decisions about important issues).

- Use strategies to fill gaps in knowledge (e.g., connecting with experts on a topic; seeking information in a library; using search engines to find additional information).

- Maintain openness to updating one's own views when presented with new facts or evidence.

These and other ML competencies can be taught and applied in any subject area because ML teaches students *how* to think, not *what* to think. Experts suggest that the best way to teach ML across K-12 settings is by incorporating it into content areas throughout the school day. Using this approach, students receive repeated exposure to the focal concepts and see ML applied to a variety of topics (Huguet, Kavanagh, et al., 2019). We hope that these connections to ML competencies will inspire teachers to seek additional ways to incorporate ML into their classrooms every day.

Overview of the Lesson Plans

These sequenced lesson plans are intended to support student engagement in public policy and equip them to resist misinformation and disinformation. We have designed five lessons that help students understand what public policy is, how it relates to their own lives, and why it is important to learn about public policy topics from credible sources. Relatedly, all lessons incorporate activities to build Truth Decay–related ML competencies in students, particularly their ability to critically consume and create information about policy topics. The lessons build on one another, and we suggest that teachers deliver them in sequence, as outlined in Table 1. Each lesson refers to worksheets to guide student learning. See Appendix A for all student worksheets.

Table 1. Lessons at a Glance

Lesson	Student Learning Objectives	Activity Overview
1	■ Students will be able to explain the meaning of terms: credibility, policy, public policy, and research. ■ Students will be able to make connections between public policy topics and their own lives.	During this first lesson, educators will ask students to select from four policy-relevant topics that they would like to learn more about as a class or in groups. Specifically, the lesson plans feature four topics related to public policy: climate change, immigration, the COVID-19 pandemic, and school start times and their impact on sleep. Our selection of these topics was based on prior research into the policy issues that teenagers care about (Garcia, Levinson, and Gaigroetzi, 2020) and on our own experience piloting these lessons with two diverse groups of middle school students in Boston, Massachusetts, and Los Angeles, California.
2	■ Students will be able to explain why an information source on a public policy topic is credible. ■ Students will be able to discuss ways that public policies can help address specific societal problems and how public policy can affect their lives.	In the second lesson, students learn about one selected policy-relevant topic by watching a recorded interview of a RAND expert on that topic and/or reading a question-and-answer policy brief with the expert in written format.
3	■ Students will be able to explain why it is important to understand who created a message, the intent behind a message, and how that might influence the credibility of the information being presented. ■ Students will be able to use a search engine to find credible information that answers a specific question they have about a public policy topic.	In third lesson, students further unpack the concept of credibility and complete an exercise to help them find credible information about their selected public policy topic using a search engine.
4	■ Students will be able to discuss intentional and unintentional consequences of sharing information that is not credible. ■ Students will be able to create a product (brief video or podcast) that communicates information about a public policy topic.	In the fourth lesson, students work on a team project (a brief video or podcast) to create an information product in which they share fact-based information about what they learned.
5	■ Students will be able to create a product (brief video or podcast) that communicates information about a public policy topic. ■ Students will be able to describe how a public policy topic relates to their own lives. ■ Students will be able to make suggestions about policies that they think would be useful, relevant to their selected topic.	In the fifth lesson, students work with their teams to present an information product in which they share fact-based information about their focal public policy topic.

NOTE: Teachers should adjust the length and pacing of these lessons to fit their classroom needs, including delivering each lesson across multiple class periods if needed.

Focusing on Students in Grades 6–8

The lesson plans are designed for use with students in grades 6–8 (typically ages 11–13). We selected these grades because preadolescence and early adolescence represent a critical juncture in human development during which youth increasingly shift away from family and toward peers and the outside world. During this age, youth are still forming their behavioral patterns, including how they consume media (Webb and Martin, 2012). It is also during this period that most youth create social media accounts; a recent survey found that 78 percent of youth created social media accounts between the ages of 10 and 13, which increases their potential exposure to misinformation and disinformation (Martin et al., 2018).[1] Thus, it is essential to improve middle school students' ability to resist misinformation and disinformation and to increase their exposure to public policy research that could counter inaccurate or misleading information they might be confronted with online. Furthermore, by encouraging young students' engagement with policy-relevant research, we also hope to spark their interests in pursuing classes, activities, or careers in the fields of public policy, science, and social science.

Lessons Connect to Multiple Subject Areas

We designed the lesson plans so that teachers can incorporate them into a variety of subject areas and in different settings. The content of the lesson plans connects to different subject areas and to instruction in afterschool settings in the following ways:

- The focus on public policy and policy-relevant topics makes the lesson plans relevant for integration into social studies and/or civic education classes.

- The inclusion of nonfiction texts and activities related to reading comprehension and writing can also allow teachers to incorporate these lessons into English Language Arts classes (see Appendix B for links to relevant standards).

- The use of inquiry-based learning tasks and references to research could also allow science

teachers to use these lessons in classes related to the scientific process, especially if they were to focus on the topics of sleep, COVID-19, and/or climate change.

- The lessons can also be used by those teaching media classes, given the inclusion of Truth Decay–related ML competencies and the option for students to create an information product, such as a video or podcast.

- The use of project-based learning and student choice could also allow afterschool providers to deliver the lesson plans to groups of middle school students.

In addition, Appendix B lists the specific standards and competencies that the lessons cover, including CCSS, the Truth Decay Media Literacy Standards (Huguet, Baker, et al., 2021a), the P21 Framework for 21st Century Learning Competencies (Battelle for Kids, undated), and a Next Generation Science Standard (Next Generation Science Standards, undated).

Suggested Instructional Strategies

We intentionally integrated instructional strategies that are backed by research. For example, *know–want to know–learn* charts (introduced in Lesson One) are examples of advance organizers; their use has been associated with helping students draw on their existing knowledge to learn new information (Clemons et al., 2010). However, because research has not yet provided causal evidence linking these instructional strategies with student achievement or civic outcomes, we refer to these strategies as "promising" rather than "proven" or "best" practices. Although most of the instructional strategies that we use in the lesson plans are widely used and likely familiar to teachers, we provide brief descriptions of each to facilitate their use by newer educators or instructors in other settings, such as afterschool programs.

---

[1] *Misinformation* is a claim that "contradicts or distorts common understanding of verifiable facts" (Guess and Lyons, 2020, p. 10). *Disinformation* is misinformation that is spread to deliberately mislead.

Strategies to Assess Student Learning

We provide some options for assessment in the lesson plans. We incorporate informal end-of-lesson assessments that we call "exit tickets." These are intended to provide quick opportunities for teachers to check in on the degree to which students grasp the concepts introduced in the lesson. Ideally, student responses on these formative assessments will inform the subsequent lesson; teachers can adapt their instruction by revisiting concepts and clarifying ideas or restructuring activities for better delivery in future lessons (Fowler, Windschitl, and Richards, 2019).

The culminating task requires students to create an information product. We provide a simple rubric that teachers can use to evaluate the product. Rubrics establish guidelines that promote consistency in learning expectations (Jonsson and Svingby, 2007). The simplicity of our rubric helps make criteria for success on the assignment clear to students. If teachers are inclined, they can revise the rubric tool using student input, a technique that might improve students' ownership of the task (Ghaffar, Khairallah, and Salloum, 2020). Alternatively, they can adapt the rubric to align it with other rubrics or criteria with which students are familiar and that are aligned to district or state standards.

Both types of assessment provided in the lesson plans—exit tickets and the project rubric—are suggestions. These are research-based strategies, but the specific lessons and assessments listed here have not been evaluated for effectiveness themselves. We also encourage teachers to use ongoing informal assessment strategies during the course of the lesson plans; for instance, teachers may choose to use quick "thumbs-up, thumbs-down" activities to ask students if they are understanding concepts throughout a lesson.

Adjusting Lessons for Teacher and Student Needs

To assist teachers, we provide several callout boxes providing instructional strategies (shaded in gray). However, teachers know their students best; we therefore suggest that teachers adapt activities and tasks to best meet the needs of their students. For this reason, we add options and opportunities throughout the plans for teachers to make the lessons their own. For instance, throughout the lesson plans, we provide callout boxes that provide variations in lesson delivery (shaded in green), and we also provide example responses that teachers can use to facilitate discussions, but these are only options. We also provide several callout boxes (shaded in blue) throughout the lessons that teachers can use to extend the conversations in the lessons and add complexity, if scheduling allows.

In addition, we compiled suggestions for teachers working with students who have specific needs. In Appendix C, we make suggestions for how to scaffold learning for English learners and to address learning needs linked to general learning disabilities; these suggestions might be helpful for all learners, independent of their identification for special education services. In addition to reviewing our suggested supports for special populations, teachers can consult the relevant sources to decide whether and how to implement these supports for their students.

Lesson One

What Is Public Policy?

Objectives

- Students will be able to explain the meaning of terms: credibility, policy, public policy, and research.

- Students will be able to make connections between public policy topics to their own lives.

Materials

- Students will need a writing utensil and the Lesson One worksheet in the student packet (Appendix A). We recommend giving the worksheets to students as a packet, but they could also be distributed day by day.

- Instructors will need a space to write where students can see (e.g., a computer and projector, white board, chalk board). We will refer to this as *the board*, although it is flexible to the classroom.

- Suggested lesson time is 60 minutes.

Preview for Students

Give students an outline of where these five lessons will be taking them. One option for previewing the lesson arc might consist of the following:

- *In today's lesson, we will talk about something new to us called policy. Policies are rules, laws, or guidelines, and public policies are rules, laws, or guidelines created by government.*

A Do Now is an instructional strategy that teachers can use as part of their daily routines to help students focus on a new activity after a class transition. The strategy consists of giving students a quick activity to do as soon as they arrive in the class. If implemented daily, students will know what to do when arriving in the classroom or transitioning to a different subject without needing teachers to direct them to the activity (ABLconnect, undated).

- *In the next lesson, we will learn more about a public policy topic, and you all get to select the public policy topic you want to learn about.*

- *In the third lesson, we will learn more about how we can better identify whether the information we read online is trustworthy, and we will apply what we learned by doing an online search to answer our questions about that same public policy topic.*

- *In the fourth lesson, we'll talk about how to take accurate information that we learned and share it with people we know.*

- *In the final lesson, you all will actually share what you learned about a public policy topic with your classmates.*

Lesson Components

Do Now (8 minutes)

Vocabulary: Credible

Introduce the following questions to begin the lesson, and ask students to write their answers on their worksheet:

- *If your friend broke their arm while playing, where do you think they should go for help? Why?*

- *If you wanted to find out if your favorite sports team won a game last night, where should you look for that information? Why?*

After students have individually completed their answers in the Lesson One worksheet, ask them to **think-pair-share** and discuss their responses with a neighbor. Select a few students to share their responses out loud.

If similar answers are not already provided by students, redirect the conversation with your own responses. Options include the following:

- *If a friend were to break an arm, they should go to the hospital, where they could see a doctor. I know that a hospital is a place that takes care of people, and doctors have years of education to help them provide reliable care.*

- *If I wanted to know what the scores were for a sports game last night, I should go to a well-known website or newspaper that covers sports. These are publications that have a lot of experience in reporting scores, they will post scores that are up-to-date, and it benefits them to report accurately.*

Think-pair-share is an instructional strategy that involves asking students to: (1) think quietly about an open-ended question for a set time; (2) turn to a partner or nearby student to discuss the questions for two to five minutes; and (3) then share what they discussed with their partners with the rest of the class (Lyman, 1981).

Write the word *credible* on the board and explain that people and organizations can be more or less credible. Write the definition for *credible* next to the word on the board, and ask students to write it down on their Lesson One worksheet, in the top left-hand corner of the vocabulary box:

Experienced, knowledgeable, and reliable in a specific topic

Then, discuss examples of people or sources that we typically consider to be credible in different topics. (Examples could include the following: A chef would be credible giving you instructions about how to make a pizza.

A mechanic would be credible in telling you how to fix a problem with your car.) Ask students to write their own examples in their vocabulary boxes. We recommend having students complete this activity in groups or pairs to make it more interactive, then sharing as a class.

Introducing Public Policy (25 minutes)

Vocabulary: Policy, public policy, and research

Explain that there are two more vocabulary terms that students will learn today: *policy* and *public policy*. Ask students if they know what these terms mean, and discuss as a class.

Write the definitions on the board, and ask students to write them down the following on their Lesson One worksheet:

- *Policy: A guideline, rule, or law*

- *Public policy: A guideline, rule, or law created by government*

Explain that people in government at many different levels make public policies, and these policies can affect different aspects of our lives. *Government* can mean local government, such as supervisors in a school district, all the way up to the national government, such as lawmakers in Congress.

Give your own examples of policies that students might know about, and help students distinguish between policy and public policy, asking them for examples. The following are potential examples to get started:

- Policy: Our classroom has a policy about respecting other people's opinions (if true).

- Policy: Stores have policies about whether you can return items.

- Public policy: A policymaker at the local, state, or national level (i.e., the state department of education) can decide what students learn about in school.

- Public policy: Policymakers also decide how old you have to be to get a driver's license or a job.

Tell students to write their examples in the correct vocabulary boxes to show they know how public policy is different from policy generally.

Ask students: *Why do you think governments make public policies? Let's think about state regulations that say we have to wear seatbelts while driving or when you are a passenger in a car. Why do we have that policy?* Allow students to think-pair-share, then ask for responses.

After students have responded, move on to discuss the seatbelt policy topic. We recommend introducing the excerpt (located in their Lesson One worksheet) by explaining the following: *This is taken from an article written by a credible source, which is the Centers for Disease Control and Prevention (CDC). The CDC is a government agency and its main goal is to protect the safety and health of all the people living in our country. This agency is responsible for tracking many topics related to health, and it writes guidelines that can help us stay safe. The information in the article is credible because it contains references to research written by many different people with different*

Adding Complexity:
Have a classroom discussion about whether policies are always fair or right. Ask students for examples and evidence to support their perspectives.

You could also, or instead, have a classroom discussion imagining what would happen in a world without guidelines, rules, or laws. What would students like about this, and what would they not like?

The **vocabulary box** we use is a shortened adaptation of the Frayer model. This model is used to introduce concepts in ways that provide context for new vocabulary (Frayer, Frederick, and Klausmeier, 1969). If there is time, teachers might want to add *characteristics* and *non-examples* to the discussion, to be more aligned with the original design of the model.

kinds of relevant expertise, and their motivation is to keep you safe and healthy.

As a class, read the brief excerpt about seatbelts from the Centers for Disease Control (CDC, 2020). Students have a copy on their worksheet:

In the United States, car accidents are a leading cause of death among people who are 1–54 years old.[a] Young adults who are 18–24 years old are less likely to wear seatbelts than people who are older.[b] Seat belt use is one of the most effective ways to save lives and reduce injuries in car accidents.[c] Based on data from the National Highway Traffic Safety Administration, seat belts save almost 15,000 lives per year.[d] In most states—but not all—drivers can be pulled over and given a ticket if they are not wearing a seatbelt.

[a] Centers for Disease Control and Prevention, *WISQARS (Web-Based Injury Statistics Query and Reporting System)*, Atlanta, Ga.: U.S. Department of Health and Human Services, database, 2015. As of September 2, 2020: https://www.cdc.gov/injury/wisqars/index.html

[b] Laurie F. Beck, Jonathan Downs, Mark R. Stevens, and Erin K. Sauber-Schatz, "Rural and Urban Differences in Passenger-Vehicle–Occupant Deaths and Seat Belt Use Among Adults—United States, 2014," *Morbidity and Mortality Weekly Report*, Vol. 66, No. SS-17, 2017.

c National Highway Traffic Safety Administration, *Lives Saved in 2017 by Restraint Use and Minimum-Drinking-Age Laws*, Washington, D.C.: U.S. Department of Transportation, Publication no. DOT-HS-812-683, 2019.

d National Highway Traffic Safety Administration, 2019.

Then, with the class, complete the "Understanding Public Policy: Car Accidents and Seatbelts" activity. Consider completing this activity so that students can watch you fill in the worksheet as they volunteer answers (e.g., on a projector screen), or have students complete the worksheet in their groups and then come together as a class to discuss. The following are some example responses to these questions:

1. **Topic:** Car accidents and seatbelts

2. **Is there a problem related to this topic that policy could fix? What is the problem?**
   People can get very hurt in car accidents.

3. **How can policy help fix this problem?**
   The government can require people to wear seatbelts. If you don't wear a seatbelt, you can get a ticket.

4. **How do I know public policy about this topic can make a difference?**
   Research shows that wearing seatbelts can save lives and reduce injuries.

5. **How does this topic relate to me and other kids my age?**
   [Discuss student responses as a class]

Talk with students about why policymakers might want to use credible information to make policies. Provide an example, such as the following:

If the government is making a policy about seatbelts, like we read about here, it would be good to base it in credible information. For example, government officials making policy about seatbelts might want to know how seatbelts can help decrease injuries, and officials need to be able to find reliable, trustworthy facts about this topic. That is why we see all of these references at the bottom of the page—the references are to research studies that the CDC identified as providing important information about seatbelts and safety.

Write the word *research* on the board and ask students what they think the word means. Take a few responses from students. Then, write the definition on the board, and ask students to fill in their vocabulary squares.

Research: an organized approach to discovering or explaining new knowledge

Discuss this definition with students. *Organized* means that there is a plan and a system to learning something new. The experts from whom the students will be hearing in the next lesson are researchers, and they study different things, but all of them use a careful process; they formulate questions and plan a way to find the answers using techniques specific to their field. Provide a few examples of research (e.g., zoologists observing animals to learn more about their behaviors; climate scientists measuring

Adding Complexity:
Have a classroom discussion about what other kinds of information might inform policies, in addition to credible facts and research. Some examples might be

- the cost of starting and maintaining a policy

- popular sentiment—do people like the idea?

Voting is an instructional strategy that creates opportunities for students to make specific choices about the academic content they will learn or how they will learn about it. Incorporating student choice into instruction can set democratic norms in the classroom and help students take responsibility for their own learning. (Yoder and Gurke, 2017).

the amount of rainfall that falls in a specific place every year; doctors testing new medicines). Then, ask students to think-pair-share and fill in examples in their vocabulary squares in the Lesson One worksheet; share a few student examples as a class.

Selecting Policy-Relevant Topics, Building Interest (25 minutes)

Students in the class will vote to select one of four policy topics that they are interested in learning more about. As the instructor, provide as much or as little information about the topics as you would like (some brief information is in Table 2). In the next lesson, students will be learning more about their selected topic by watching a recorded interview of a RAND expert on that topic and/or reading a Q&A document with the expert in written format.

One way to introduce the topics that students will choose from could be the following example:

As we discussed earlier, public policies are often created to keep people safe and healthy, increase people's well-being, and address problems that we are facing as a society. That means many topics that people care about or that you hear about in the news are related to policy, such as climate change, immigration, and the COVID-19 pandemic. Policies can even influence how much sleep we get, which affects our health.

Present the four policy topic options to students. Tallying on the board, ask students to vote just once for whichever topic they are most interested in learning about. Once tallied, confirm with the students which topic the class

Table 2. Introducing the Four Public Policy Topics From Which Students Can Choose

Topic	Short Introduction to Each Topic And Its Relation to Public Policy
Climate change	*Climate change* refers to long-term changes in the world's temperature, which has gotten warmer in the past 70 years. This increase in temperature was mainly caused by human activities, such as driving cars, and has caused such problems as droughts. Governments can help slow climate change by making public policies to help reduce some of the activities that cause climate change. For example, governments can determine that cars that emit too much carbon dioxide can no longer be made (Hubbe and Hubbe, 2019).
COVID-19	Coronavirus disease 2019, or COVID-19 for short, is a disease caused by a virus called severe acute respiratory syndrome coronavirus 2 (or SARS- CoV-2). The disease can cause such symptoms as fever, cough, and trouble breathing. It spreads easily and has now affected people across the world. Public policies about vaccinations, testing, and mask wearing can help communities slow the spread of the virus and prevent serious illness (Tomlin, 2021).
Immigration	There are 281 million migrants in the world. These are people who have moved from the country where they were born to a new country. Most countries in the world require people to get permission to enter and have public policies about how many people can enter a country, for how long, and for what reasons (International Organization for Migration, 2020).
School start times and their impact on sleep	Sleep is very important for our health and well-being. For example, not getting enough sleep can make it more difficult for us to concentrate in school, and it can make us get sick more easily. Unfortunately, most teens do not get enough sleep. However, school district policies could help students get more sleep by changing school start times (Troxel, 2020)

will focus on. Ask students to write the topic on the top of page 8 of Lesson 1 in the packet.

Ask students what, if anything, they know about the topic they selected, how they learned about the topic, and how it affects them or relates to their lives. Call on respondents. As students volunteer their knowledge, write what they are saying on the board, and have students complete the first column of the **know–want to know–learn chart** in their Lesson One worksheet. As students discuss what they already know and how they learned about the topic, ask them questions to identify if their knowledge comes from *credible* sources or if what they think they already know may actually belong in the second column: what they *want* to know about the topic.

Then, ask students what they *want* to know about the topic. What questions do they have? As students volunteer questions, write them on the board, and ask students to record them on the second column of the know–want to know–learn chart. Students will be completing the third column in a later lesson, so ask them to keep the worksheet/packet in a safe place.

If students are having difficulty responding to either of these queries, ask them again to think about it with a partner or in a group. Afterward, ask the question again and share with the class.

Closing (2 minutes)

Tell students that they will learn more about this policy topic in the next lesson, so they should keep their questions in mind.

On the **exit ticket** on their worksheet, ask students to write down an example of a *public* policy not already discussed in class and how it relates to their own lives. Checking these exit tickets will provide input about how well students understood some of the key concepts at the center of the lesson.

The exit ticket for Lesson One is as follows:

■ *Write down an example of a public policy that we have not already discussed, and describe how it relates to your life.*

Checking these exit tickets will provide input about how well students understood some of the key concepts at the center of the lesson.

Varying Lesson Delivery: Instead of selecting one policy topic as a class, you may choose to have groups of students focus on different topics of interest. If using this approach, students will be able to teach the other groups about their topics during the final lesson. If groups select different topics, have them complete their know–want to know–learn charts in their groups.

Know–want to know–learn is a strategy that encourages students to think about what they already know about a particular issue, what they would like to find out, and what they have learned after reading a text or completing an activity. To help students reflect on these questions and record their answers, they can use a chart like the one in Worksheet One in Appendix A (Ogle, 1989).

Exit tickets are short-response tasks given to students at the end of a lesson or activity. Student responses can provide educators with evidence of whether students understood the concepts covered in a lesson or whether there are any misunderstandings. The activity can also help students reflect on their understanding of content (Fowler, Windschitl, and Richards, 2019).

Lesson Two

Learning About Public Policy Topics from Credible Sources

Objective

- Students will be able to explain why an information source on a public policy topic is credible.

- Students will be able to discuss ways that public policies can help address specific societal problems, and how public policy can affect their lives.

Materials

- Expert Q&A documents

- Videos with experts, and technology to play the videos in class (optional)

- Students will need a writing utensil and the Lesson One and Two worksheets in the student packet (Appendix A).

- Instructors will need a space to write where students can see (e.g., a computer and projector, white board, chalk board). We will refer to this as *the board* although it is flexible to the classroom.

- Suggested lesson time: 60 minutes

Note: The next three lessons suggest that students work in groups of four to five students. Consider how your students would best be grouped to accomplish a creative project. If grouping is not feasible for your class, consider placing students in pairs.

Lesson Components

Do Now (10 minutes)

Start class by passing out the expert Q&A document that corresponds with the topic selected by students, and previewing the lesson's activities. For example:

As we voted on in the previous lesson, today we will begin learning about [policy topic]. Last time, you wrote down some questions you have about the policy topic. Today, we are going to learn about this topic from a credible expert who conducts research on that topic.

Next, ask students to read the expert's bio on the Q&A document. Ask students for some reasons why this person might be credible. Some possible answers are:

- They have been studying this topic for a long time (experience).
- They have received degrees related to this topic from universities (education).

Explain to students that the class will be listening to a credible expert discuss the policy-related topic that they selected last week. The video is an example of the kind of information that could be useful to share about a public policy topic (because it comes from a credible expert sharing facts). Remind students that, even when listening to people who appear to be credible, it is important to consider whether the information they are sharing is credible.

*Note about information on COVID-19: The video and Q&A document about COVID-19 were created in early 2022. Given that researchers' understanding of COVID-19 has changed during different phases of the pandemic, we suggest that educators discuss the importance of paying attention to **when** information was published in thinking about credibility of different information sources. See the "Adding Complexity" box on the left for a suggestion about how to discuss this topic with your students.*

Watching Policy Expert Interviews (15 minutes)

If your classroom does not have technology to watch the video, skip this portion and begin with reading the expert Q&A. If groups are working on different policy topics, complete the video portion of the lesson in groups as opposed to with the whole class.

Before beginning, tell students to write down information that they learn from the video in the last column of their know–want to know–learn chart in the Lesson One worksheet. Each student should write down facts that they learn and additional questions that they have about the policy topic. Ask students to think about ways that this policy topic might be related to their own lives.

Watch the interview with the class. Recap the video with students afterward as follows:

- Ask students what new information they learned.

- Ask students if any of the information they thought they knew—written in the first column of the know–want to know–learn chart—was incorrect.

- Ask students to cross out the incorrect information and add what they learned to their charts. Note that it is important that we can update our viewpoint when we learn new, credible information.

Reviewing the Written Q&A (35 minutes)

After the video, assign students to work in groups of four or five (if this has not already been done), and ask students to take out the Q&A document that they used to read about the expert. Students should now read the expert Q&A. There are multiple approaches for reading the document, including the following suggestions:

- Instruct students to take turns reading paragraphs in their groups as you visit groups to engage with them.

- Instruct students to select one person to be the interviewer and the others to be policy "experts." The interviewer will read a question to each expert, and the experts will read the answers.

- Organize a **jigsaw** activity in which students read different portions of the text and then share with one another what they learned.

- You could also read the expert Q&A as a full class, with different students reading brief sections.

Regardless of how students read the brief, instruct them to underline facts that they think are important in understanding *what the problem is related to the topic, and how policy could help fix this problem.* Students can also **annotate** the Q&A document to identify key words and to make note of questions that they have about the topic.

After the class has completed the reading, which echoes the video, ask them to work in their groups to answer the questions on the Lesson Two worksheets in the student packet. Students can reference the notes that they took during the video (in their know–want to know–learn charts), and their annotated expert Q&A document. Once they have finished answering the questions—one of which asks students to identify ways that the policy topic is relevant to their own lives—bring the class together. Call on groups to share their responses to the questions with the class.

A **jigsaw** generally involves the following steps:

- The teacher divides a task or source material (i.e., the expert Q&A) into parts and assigns students to read/ complete different parts.

- Students individually read/complete their assigned parts.

- Students assigned the same part are asked to discuss their understanding of it and become the "expert group" in that part in order to present or explain it to other students.

- Students then get into their "jigsaw" group, which consists of one representative from each of the "expert groups," and take turns presenting their piece of the task/source material (Aronson et al., 1978).

Annotation is a useful strategy to help students engage as they read a text. There are many ways to annotate a text; examples include asking students to draw a circle around key words, underline important facts or main ideas, and make notes on the margins of a text to flag confusing information or jot down their questions (Zywica and Gomez, 2008).

Closing (5 minutes)

Tell students that in the next class they will be working to answer any new or unanswered questions about the public policy topic by looking for credible information about the topic online.

This lesson's exit ticket asks students to answer the following question:

- *Why do you think it is important to learn about the policy topic, and the public policies related to this topic, from credible, fact-based information sources?*

Lesson Three

Finding Credible Information About Public Policy Topics

Objective

- Students will be able to explain why it is important to understand who created a message, the intent behind a message, and how that may influence the credibility of the information being presented.

- Students will be able to use a search engine to find credible information that answers a specific question they have about a public policy topic.

Materials

- Students will need a writing utensil and the Lesson One, Two, and Three worksheets in the student packet (Appendix A).

- Students will need access to computers and internet.

- Instructors will need a space to write where students can see (e.g., a computer and projector, white board, chalk board). We will refer to this as *the board*, although it is flexible to the classroom.

- Suggested lesson time: 60 minutes

Note: This lesson requires computers and internet access and assumes that the classroom already has established rules related to internet usage. If your class has not established norms related to internet usage, please do so prior to this lesson.

Alternative for classes without access to multiple computers with internet access: If your class does not have access to computers, you can skip this lesson and move to Lesson Four. Alternatively, you could adapt the lesson so that you can conduct a similar exercise without needing access to multiple computers for students. The first activity, "Messages Are Constructed for a Purpose," can be completed as long as your class has access to one computer with internet access. If you do not, you can conduct the suggested activity prior to class and print out materials for students to read. You will then adjust the activity so that students are looking at printouts instead of the results of a search engine. The second activity requires that students have access to computers, but you can also modify this activity so that it becomes a whole-class activity or you can again gather printed materials prior to class for students to use as references instead of relying on access to a search engine.

Lesson Components

Do Now (10 minutes)

Introduce the following questions to begin the lesson, and ask students to write their answers on their Lesson Three worksheet (they will also need to reference the know–want to know–learn chart in the Lesson One worksheet):

- *What surprising new information did you learn from watching the Q&A video and reading the Q&A document?*

- *Did you have to change anything in your "know" column and update your prior beliefs?*

As students get started, model responses by providing an example of what surprised you from what you saw in the previous lesson and how you updated your prior beliefs, if at all. After students have individually completed their answers, ask them to think-pair-share and discuss their responses with a neighbor. Select a few students to share their responses out loud.

Messages Are Constructed for a Purpose (15 mins)

Begin the lesson by providing students with the following information:

- *All information that we receive—whether it is on the television, in the newspaper, or on our social media feeds—is created by a person or an organization with a point of view and a reason to share the information.*

Ask students: *What are some good reasons why people might share information with others?* Discuss their responses. Some options are: Researchers want to inform the public about important new findings; doctors want to share information that would protect their patients' health.

Then ask students: *What are some self-interested reasons why people might share information with others?* Discuss their responses. Some options are: They might want to sell you something; they may want to create confusion.

- *When seeking information, especially online, you want to think about who is creating a message and try to understand why. If people are motivated by negative reasons, their information may not be as trustworthy.*

Tell students that you will be doing some searching online to answer at least one question that they have remaining about the policy topic. They will seek answers online, and each time they visit a new website, they should ask themselves two questions (excerpted from the Center for Media Literacy, 2005; Jolls and Wilson, 2014):

1. *Who created this message?*

2. *Why did they create this message?*

If students determine that the person who created the message may be primarily motivated by their own interests (e.g., selling a product or gaining influence), they should seek additional confirmation from other sources.

Next, ask students to turn to their answers to Question 5 in the Lesson Two worksheet (where students identified new and unanswered questions about the public policy topic; students may also need to reference the know–want to know–learn chart in the Lesson One worksheet). Ask volunteers to share some of the questions that they have with the class.

Pick one of the questions that students offer and write it where they can see. You will model searching online for an answer, asking the two questions about who created the message and why.

Think aloud as you enter the policy-relevant question into a search engine and analyze the results. Click on sites that may provide the answer, and model out loud asking the two questions: (1) Who created this message? and (2) Why did they create this message? It would also be illustrative to intentionally visit some sites that are *not* helpful, such as a site that is selling a product. Provide your responses to these questions, but also ask for students' perspectives. Complete this task with several websites, increasingly leaning on students to answer the questions.

End the activity by confirming an answer to the policy-relevant question with the class. On the board, write the answer, the websites that provided the information to you, and why the information found on the website is credible (you can organize this information using the table in the Lesson Three handout as an example).

Students Seek Answers to Remaining Questions (30 minutes)

Ask students to revisit their answers to Question 5 in the Lesson Two worksheet and select one of the questions or topics that they want to know more about. If this is not already framed in question form, help them turn it into one. (For instance, a topic of "ice caps" could be turned into a question: "What is happening to the ice caps?")

Tell students to repeat the process that you just modeled with the class and answer at least one of their questions with information that they think is reliable. You might choose to have students do this task individually or in their groups. As students work, provide guidance about asking the two questions—Who created this message? Why did they create this message?—and remind them to write down the website that they borrow information from.

Instruct students to write down an answer to their policy-relevant question in the Lesson Three worksheet. Not all questions that the students pose will have easily accessible answers. If they are unable to craft a direct answer based on their search, ask them to write down follow-up questions.

At the end of the allotted time, bring students back together. Reflect on what they found challenging about seeking information online, and asking questions about the information sources.

Continuing the Conversation:

This lesson is only a condensed introduction to the concept that all messages are constructed, a central tenet of ML. One lesson will not equip students to use these skills in their everyday lives. Consider ways that you can integrate these ideas into your regular activities, so that students see them repeated in different ways. For full information related to the questions excerpted here, see The Center for Media Literacy's "Five Key Questions of Media Literacy" (2005).

Adding Complexity:

Citing existing work is important. We do not provide instructions on citations in this brief lesson plan series, but numerous other sources can support your work in that area.

Have a discussion with students: Why is it important that we give credit when we use information that someone else has put into the world?

Closing (5 minutes)

Tell students that in the next class, they will be creating brief videos or podcasts to share information that they learned about how their public policy topics relate to them and other students their age, and how public policy can play a role in fixing a problem or problems.

On an exit ticket, instruct students to answer the following question:

- *Why does it matter **who** created a message?*

Lesson Four

Creating Information Products

Objective

- Students will be able to discuss intentional and unintentional consequences of sharing information that is not credible.

- Students will be able to create a product (brief video or podcast) that communicates information about a public policy topic.

Materials

- Expert Q&A document

- Students will need a writing utensil and the Lesson Four worksheet in the student packet (Appendix A).

- Instructors will need a space to write where students can see (e.g., a computer and projector, white board, chalk board). We will refer to this as *the board* although it is flexible to the classroom.

- Suggested lesson time: 60 minutes

Lesson Components

Do Now (10 minutes)

If possible, set up the two tweets (displayed here) that are included in students' packets to be projected where students can view them. Remind

---

Suggested creation of information products and no-technology alternatives

We suggest creating brief videos (similar to TikTok) or podcasts in student groups because these are options that are relevant to students in middle school grades at the time of publication. It would be fine to make different kinds of information products that could hypothetically be shared online. We do not advocate actually sharing these products.

We discuss these information products as if you have access to technology such as smart phones, video recorders, or audio recorders for students to use. However, this activity can also be completed without any technology at all; students could create a presentation or perform for the class without ever recording.

Another Option: When you leave one website to see what other websites/sources have to say about it, this is called *lateral reading*.

There are several research-based lateral reading lessons available for free via the Stanford History Education Group (undated).

Resources for video/podcast creation

We assume that teachers and students have some knowledge about how to create brief videos or how to record a podcast on a computer or audio recorder. However, educators can also incorporate or add other lessons on media creation as needed. Helpful and free sources for information and guidance on video/podcast creation:

"Teaching Podcasting: A Curriculum Guide for Educators" (NPR, 2018)

"KQED Media Academy for Educators" (KQED, undated)

"Shout Out: A Kid's Guide to Recording Stories" (Davis, 2013)

students to ask their two questions: Who created this message? Why did they create the message? Then ask,

Do you find the information in each of these tweets credible? Why or why not?

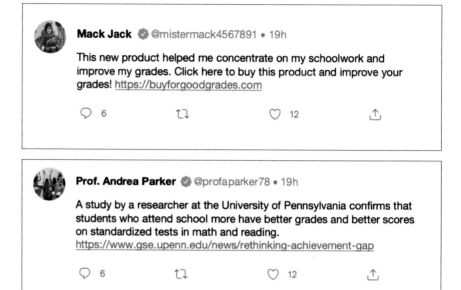

After allowing students time to write their answers, call on students for responses. Guide the conversation to explain the following:

- One of the tweets refers to a study (likely more credible, though you would want to find out more about the study).

- One of the tweets has a person's name, while the other seems to be a made-up name.

- One of the tweets looks like it might be trying to sell something, meaning they might have interest in convincing you in order to make money (making it less credible).

- One of the tweets is providing more of an opinion than a fact (making it less credible).

Explain to students that if they were to come across tweets like this in real life, it would be helpful to open another browser window and search for other information that also says the information in the tweet is accurate. For example, they could search for the name of the person posting the tweet to make sure the person exists, has relevant experience and/or is affiliated with a credible institution. They can also search for "does school attendance improve grades?" in a search engine to see if additional sources confirm the information.

Tell students that unfortunately, not everyone shares *credible* information online. *Sometimes people share information that is not based on facts, research, or reality but is instead meant to manipulate you into thinking, believing, or doing something. On a big scale, this can have negative consequences for our world.* Give some examples (you may use the following options or your own):

- Pretend someone posted an article online that said cigarettes are not bad for you. We know cigarettes are unhealthy and can damage our bodies. What are the consequences of sharing this article? (Sample responses: People might begin smoking, or not quit smoking, because they believed what the article said.)

- Someone didn't want to go to school the next day, so they made up a story that school was canceled. They posted it on a website, where a lot of other students liked and reposted it. What could be the consequences of sharing this made-up information? (Sample responses: Students might not go to school the next day, wouldn't learn, it could hurt their grades, etc.)

In the next activity, students will have an opportunity to create an information product, such as a video or podcast. (See the earlier note about no-technology alternatives for this activity.)

Introduce Rubric (10 minutes)

Explain to students that they are going to create information products, such as a brief video or podcast, using credible information that will help other students their age better understand: (1) how the public policy topic relates to their own lives and (2) what kinds of public policies related to this topic would be useful (i.e., a student-level "policy recommendation"). Specifically, students can present information about how public policies could help slow climate change, provide better education for immigrant children, help teens get more sleep, or prevent the spread of COVID-19. The information products that students create will be based on the video and written Q&A document, as well as the information they found in Lesson Three. Let the students know that they will not actually be sharing these videos/podcasts online. We suggest that students create information products that are no longer than five minutes.

Ask students: *What makes a video or podcast interesting for students your age?* Students can think-pair-share and discuss their responses with a neighbor. If students have a hard time answering this question, ask them to think about a recent video/podcast they saw/heard (this could include the suggested examples shared with the class), and consider what made it interesting. Other questions to prompt discussion are: Was the video funny, alarming, entertaining, visually appealing? Was the video sharing any facts? Can a video be fact-based and engaging at the same time? Call on students to share with the class.

Ask students to review the rubric provided on page 2 of Lesson 4 in the packet, and discuss it with them. We recommend calling on a student to read each of the requirements in the "exceeds expectations" column, then briefly discussing with the class what each means. (Creating a rubric with your students can help develop ownership of the task; you may want to make edits to the rubric collaboratively.)

Examples of short videos or podcasts and prompts to guide the creation of information products

If you would like to share with your class examples of videos or podcasts created by students, we recommend that you visit some of the resources listed below and select a couple examples that would provide students with inspiration for their work. We suggest selecting examples that connect a topic to students' lives and share fact-based information from credible sources. Feel free to find and show examples from different sources.

- Podcasts created by teenagers for the *New York Times'* Fourth Annual Podcast Contest (Learning Network, 2021)

- Student-created video projects supported by the University of Minnesota Libraries (2021)

(Continued on next page)

Examples of short videos or podcasts and prompts to guide the creation of information products (cont.)

In addition, you might want to provide students with prompts to guide the creation of the information products. Two example prompts are listed below, but you might be able to come up with more-tailored prompts using the discussions you have had with your students about the public policy topics.

- Imagine a group of students who think that climate change does not relate to them and that there is nothing we can do to slow climate change. Make a five-minute video that explains why climate change could affect their lives now or in the future and how they can propose possible public policy solutions to climate change.

- Imagine students who have a hard time going to bed and then have to get up for school in the early morning. Make a five-minute video that explains why students your age might have a hard time falling asleep, why not getting enough sleep is bad for them, and how school district policy could help students get more sleep.

Begin Work on Information Product (35 minutes)

Either allow students to select their own **roles**, or assign roles within each group to ensure that all students are participating. Some options for roles include the following:

- **Script writer/scribe:** This student will write the wording of the script for the team, as well as participate in overall planning.

- **Actor(s):** These students will read or act out the script, as well as participate in overall planning

- **Fact checker:** This student will be responsible for making sure that all of the information in the script is based in facts that the class learned about [policy topic], as well as participate in overall planning.

- **Rubric monitor:** This student will be responsible for ensuring that the group is following the rubric closely, as well as participate in overall planning.

Groupwork supports social and cognitive development, particularly when the group is engaged in a task that students could not complete individually. Assigning students **roles** within their groups can build interdependence and help ensure participation from all group members (Slavin, 2015).

Once in their roles, students can begin to write out their script, using both the notes that they took on worksheets and the research brief for reference.

If your classroom is enabled with technology, have students record their podcasts or videos in different areas of the classroom (or, if you have access and can adequately supervise, use outdoor or hallway spaces). Monitor students closely. If you do not have technology, these scripts can be performed in the next session.

Closing (5 minutes)

Check in with students about progress on their information products. If students are not able to complete the script writing and recording in one class period, this task can be assigned for homework, or worked on in an additional class period.

On an exit ticket, instruct students to answer the following question:

- *How will you make your information product (e.g., video or podcast) both **fact-based** and **engaging** for other students your age?*

Lesson Five

Sharing Information Products Responsibly

Objective

- Students will be able to create a product (brief video or podcast) that communicates information about a public policy topic.

- Students will be able to describe how a public policy topic relates to their own lives.

- Students will be able to make suggestions about policies that they think would be useful, relevant to their selected topic.

Materials

- Students' information products (if recorded as video or audio) or scripts.

- Students will need a writing utensil and the Lesson Five worksheet in the student packet (Appendix A).

- Instructors will need a space to write where students can see (e.g., a computer and projector, white board, chalk board). We will refer to this as *the board*, though it is flexible to your classroom.

- Suggested time: 60 minutes

Lesson Components

Do Now (5 minutes)

Introduce the following questions to begin the lesson:

- *What was your favorite part of making the information product?*
- *What was most challenging about making an information product that shares fact-based information?*

Students can then think-pair-share to discuss what was challenging about making a video/podcast that shared fact-based information in an engaging way. Then, select several students to share responses with the class. Ask students to write their responses in the Lesson Five worksheet.

Tell students that today they will be sharing their credible information product with the class. Before student groups begin sharing, review the rubric with students, so that they are reminded what the directions for the projects were.

Sharing Information Products (45 minutes)

Select teams to share their information products. (This is an appropriate time to review guidelines for being audience members.) Again, this may be via technology (using video or voice recording) or it may be performed live, if technology is not available.

As each team shares its product, ask the remainder of the class: *What did this video/podcast teach us about the public policy topic and how it relates to other students your age? How do you know that the information shared by your peers was credible?* Guide the discussion.

After all teams have presented, tell them to rate their own group project using the rubric on page 2 of Lesson 5 in the packet. This provides an opportunity for students to reflect on their work.

Ask them: *What would be the consequence of sharing these videos/podcasts online?* Ask students to reflect on their responses in their Lesson Five worksheet, then guide the conversation to highlight that people might learn credible information about important topics that they care about. If these videos were not based on truth, or were meant to mislead someone, there could be negative consequences to sharing online (discuss further if needed).

Ask students to think-pair-share how they can tell whether something they watch or listen to is coming from a credible source. Then, ask students to volunteer some of their answers. Sample responses include the following:

- making sure the information is coming from a credible source, such as a well-known newspaper or someone who is a known expert in the topic

- making sure that the video/podcast is sharing facts and not opinions

- making sure that the information that is being shared is also reported by other credible sources.

Closing (5 minutes)

On an exit ticket, instruct students to answer the following question:

- *Why do you think it's important to share information about this policy topic, and about related public policy, that is fact-based and from credible sources?*

Student responses will provide some indication of the degree to which they learned about identifying credible sources of information.

Appendix A. Printable Materials for Students

The following pullout consists of student packets for five lessons.

Engaging Youth with Public Policy

Student Packet

Name: _____ Date: _____

Lesson One: What is Public Policy?

Do Now:

1. If a friend broke an arm while playing, where should they go for help?

   Why?

   _____

   _____

   _____

   _____

   _____

2. If you wanted to find out if your favorite sports team won a game last night, where should you look for that information?

   Why?

   _____

   _____

   _____

   _____

   _____

Definition

_____

_____

_____

_____

_____

_____

_____

_____

_____

Examples

_____

_____

_____

_____

_____

_____

_____

_____

_____

Word
Credible

_____

_____

_____

_____

_____

_____

_____

_____

_____

_____

_____

_____

_____

_____

_____

_____

_____

_____

Definition	Examples
_____	_____
_____	_____
_____	_____
_____	_____
_____	_____
_____	_____
_____	_____
_____	_____
_____	_____
_____	_____
_____	_____
_____	_____
_____	_____
_____	_____
_____	_____

Word
Policy

Definition	Examples
_____	_____
_____	_____
_____	_____
_____	_____
_____	_____

Words
Public
Policy

Definition	Examples
_____	_____
_____	_____
_____	_____
_____	_____
_____	_____
_____	_____
_____	_____

Public Policy: Car Accidents and Seatbelts

In the United States, car accidents are a leading cause of death among people who are 1–54 years old.[1] Young adults who are 18–24 years old are less likely to wear seatbelts than people who are older.[2] Seat belt use is one of the most effective ways to save lives and reduce injuries in crashes.[3] Based on data from the National Highway Traffic Safety Administration, seat belts save almost 15,000 lives per year.[4] In most states—but not all—drivers can be pulled over and given a ticket if they are not wearing a seatbelt.

Understanding Policy:

Car Accidents and Seatbelts

1. Topic:

2. Is there a problem related to this topic that public policy could fix?
   What is the problem?

[1] Centers for Disease Control and Prevention, *WISQARS (Web-Based Injury Statistics Query and Reporting System)*, Atlanta, Ga.: U.S. Department of Health and Human Services, database, 2015. As of September 2, 2020: https://www.cdc.gov/injury/wisqars/index.html

[2] Laurie F. Beck, Jonathan Downs, Mark R. Stevens, and Erin K. Sauber-Schatz, "Rural and Urban Differences in Passenger-Vehicle–Occupant Deaths and Seat Belt Use Among Adults—United States, 2014," *Morbidity and Mortality Weekly Report*, Vol. 66, No. SS-17, 2017, pp. 1–13.

[3] National Highway Traffic Safety Administration, *Lives Saved in 2017 by Restraint Use and Minimum-Drinking-Age Laws*, Washington, D.C.: U.S. Department of Transportation, Publication no. DOT-HS-812-683, 2019. As of September 3, 2020: https://crashstats.nhtsa.dot.gov/Api/Public/ViewPublication/812683

[4] National Highway Traffic Safety Administration, 2019.

3. How can policy help fix this problem?

4. How do I know public policy about this topic can make a difference?

5. How does this policy topic relate to me and other kids my age?

Definition	Examples
_____	_____
_____	_____
_____	_____
_____	_____
_____	_____
_____	_____

Word
Research

_____	_____
_____	_____
_____	_____
_____	_____
_____	_____
_____	_____
_____	_____

Policy topic _____

Know What do I already know about this policy topic?	Want to Know What questions do I have about this policy topic?	Learned What have I learned about the policy topic?

Exit Ticket:

Write down an example of a public policy that we have not already discussed, and describe how it relates to your life.

Name: _____ Date: _____

Lesson Two: Learning About Policy from Credible Sources

Policy expert video: **Return to your Know–Want to Know–Learned** chart on page 8 of Lesson One to write down facts that you learn from the expert.

Learning About a Public Policy Topic:

1. Topic:

2. Is there a problem related to this topic that public policy could fix? What is the problem?

3. How might public policy help fix this problem?

4. How does this policy topic relate to me and other kids my age?

5. Do you have new or unanswered questions about this topic? Circle unanswered questions in the "want to know" column and write down any new questions.

Exit Ticket:

Why do you think it is important to learn about the policy topic, and the public policies related to this topic, from credible, fact-based information sources?

Name: _____ Date: _____

Lesson Three: Finding Credible Information About Public Policy Topics

Do Now:

1. What surprising new information did you learn from watching the Q&A video and reading the Q&A document?

2. Did you have to change anything in your "know" column and update your prior beliefs?

3. All messages are constructed: What questions can I ask myself when reviewing information on a website?

Write down the questions you discussed in class, below.

Question 1.

Question 2.

4. Finding credible information online: What question will you be trying to answer through your online search? Write down the question in the space below.

5. What answers did you find? In the table below, write down the answer to your question in the first column, the website where you found the information, and why you think the information that you found is credible.

Answer:	Where did you find the information to answer your question?	Why do you think the information you found is credible?

Exit Ticket:

Why does it matter who created a message?

Name: _____ Date: _____

Lesson Four: Creating Information Products

Do Now:

1. Do you find the information in each of these tweets credible? Why or why not?

Mack Jack ✓ @mistermack4567891 • 19h

This new product helped me concentrate on my schoolwork and improve my grades. Click here to buy this product and improve your grades! https://buyforgoodgrades.com

💬 6   ↻   ♡ 12   ↑

Prof. Andrea Parker ✓ @profaparker78 • 19h

A study by a researcher at the University of Pennsylvania confirms that students who attend school more have better grades and better scores on standardized tests in math and reading. https://www.gse.upenn.edu/news/rethinking-achievement-gap

💬 6   ↻   ♡ 12   ↑

_____

_____

_____

_____

_____

_____

_____

Project Rubric

	Exceeds Expectations	Meets Expectations	Needs Improvement
Information	The information product includes at least three credible facts about the topic	The information product includes at least one credible fact about the topic	The information product does not include credible facts about the topic
Connection	The information product includes at least three examples of how the policy topic relates to students	The information product includes at least one example of how the policy topic relates to students	The information product does not include examples of how the policy topic relates to students
Public policy suggestions	The information product includes at least three suggestions about how public policy could address problems related to this topic	The information product includes one suggestion about how public policy could address problems related to this topic	The information product does not include suggestions about how public policy could address problems related to this topic
Teamwork	All group members played a meaningful role in the collaboration	Most group members played a meaningful role in the collaboration	A few team members appeared to dominate the collaboration

Exit Ticket:

How will you make your information product (e.g., video or podcast) both *fact-based* and *engaging* for other students your age?

Name: _____ Date: _____

Lesson Five: Sharing Information Products

Do Now:

What was your favorite part of making the information product?
What was the most challenging? Why?

_____

_____

_____

_____

_____

_____

_____

_____

_____

_____

_____

_____

_____

Project Rubric

	Exceeds Expectations	Meets Expectations	Needs Improvement
Information	The information product includes at least three credible facts about the topic	The information product includes at least one credible fact about the topic	The information product does not include credible facts about the topic
Connection	The information product includes at least three examples of how the policy topic relates to students	The information product includes at least one example of how the policy topic relates to students	The information product does not include examples of how the policy topic relates to students
Public policy suggestions	The information product includes at least three suggestions about how public policy could address problems related to this topic	The information product includes one suggestion about how public policy could address problems related to this topic	The information product does not include suggestions about how public policy could address problems related to this topic
Teamwork	All group members played a meaningful role in the collaboration	Most group members played a meaningful role in the collaboration	A few team members appeared to dominate the collaboration

Exit Ticket:

Why do you think it's important to share information about this policy topic, and about related public policy, that is *fact-based* and from credible sources?

Appendix B. Applicable Learning Standards

RAND's Media Literacy Standards to Counter Truth Decay (Huguet, Baker, et al., 2021a)

- Recognize limitations of one's own knowledge or understanding of the facts.
- Identify the expertise (e.g., academic credential, office held, firsthand knowledge) and consider the motivations (e.g., political, financial) of the creator of an information product.
- Anticipate and monitor intended and unintended consequences of what is shared in digital spaces.
- Take action rooted in evidence (e.g., construct new knowledge, create and share media, engage in informed conversations and decisions about important issues).
- Use strategies to fill gaps in knowledge (e.g., connecting with experts on a topic, seeking information in a library, using search engines to find additional information)
- Maintain openness to updating one's own views when presented with new facts or evidence.

P21 Framework for 21st Century Learning Competencies (Battelle for Kids, undated)

- Use 21st century skills to understand and address global issues.
- Participate effectively in civic life through knowing how to stay informed and understanding governmental processes.
- Understand the local and global implications of civic decisions.
- Demonstrate knowledge and understanding of the environment and the circumstances and conditions affecting it, particularly as relates to air, climate, land, food, energy, water, and ecosystems.[a]
- Effectively analyze and evaluate evidence, arguments, claims, and beliefs.
- Reflect critically on learning experiences and processes.
- Use communication for a variety of purposes (e.g. to inform, instruct, motivate, and persuade).
- Utilize multiple media and technologies, and know how to judge their effectiveness as well as assess their impact.
- Collaborate with others.
- Demonstrate ability to work effectively and respectfully with diverse teams.
- Evaluate information critically and competently.
- Use information accurately and creatively for the issue or problem at hand.
- Understand both how and why media messages are constructed and for what purposes.
- Use technology as a tool to research, organize, evaluate, and communicate information.

Common Core State Standards, English Language Arts, Literacy, Speaking and Listening, Reading Informational Texts, Writing (Grade 6) (Common Core State Standards Initiative, 2010)

- CCSS.ELA-LITERACY.SL.6.1.B: Follow rules for collegial discussions, set specific goals and deadlines, and define individual roles as needed.

- CCSS.ELA-LITERACY.SL.6.5: Include multimedia components (e.g., graphics, images, music, sound) and visual displays in presentations to clarify information.

- CCSS.ELA-LITERACY.RI.6.7: Integrate information presented in different media or formats (e.g., visually, quantitatively) as well as in words to develop a coherent understanding of a topic or issue.

- CCSS.ELA-LITERACY.W.6.1.B: Support claim(s) with clear reasons and relevant evidence, using credible sources and demonstrating an understanding of the topic or text.

- CCSS.ELA-LITERACY.W.6.2.A: Introduce a topic; organize ideas, concepts, and information, using strategies such as definition, classification, comparison/contrast, and cause/effect; include formatting (e.g., headings), graphics (e.g., charts, tables), and multimedia when useful to aiding comprehension.

- CCSS.ELA-LITERACY.W.6.2.B: Develop the topic with relevant facts, definitions, concrete details, quotations, or other information and examples.

- CCSS.ELA-LITERACY.W.6.2.D: Use precise language and domain-specific vocabulary to inform about or explain the topic.

- CCSS.ELA-LITERACY.W.6.9: Draw evidence from literary or informational texts to support analysis, reflection, and research.

Common Core State Standards, English Language Arts, Literacy, Speaking and Listening, Writing (Grade 7) (Common Core State Standards Initiative, 2010)

- CCSS.ELA-LITERACY.SL.7.1.B: Follow rules for collegial discussions, set specific goals and deadlines, and define individual roles as needed.

- CCSS.ELA-LITERACY.SL.7.5: Include multimedia components and visual displays in presentations to clarify claims and findings and emphasize salient points.

- CCSS.ELA-LITERACY.W.7.1.B: Support claim(s) with clear reasons and relevant evidence, using credible sources and demonstrating an understanding of the topic or text.

- CCSS.ELA-LITERACY.W.7.2.A: Introduce a topic; organize ideas, concepts, and information, using strategies such as definition, classification, comparison/contrast, and cause/effect; include formatting (e.g., headings), graphics (e.g., charts, tables), and multimedia when useful to aiding comprehension.

- CCSS.ELA-LITERACY.W.7.2.B: Develop the topic with relevant facts, definitions, concrete details, quotations, or other information and examples.

- CCSS.ELA-LITERACY.W.7.2.D: Use precise language and domain-specific vocabulary to inform about or explain the topic.

- CCSS.ELA-LITERACY.W.7.9: Draw evidence from literary or informational texts to support analysis, reflection, and research.

Common Core State Standards, English Language Arts, Literacy, Speaking and Listening, Writing (Grade 8) (Common Core State Standards Initiative, 2010)

- CCSS.ELA-LITERACY.SL.8.1.B: Follow rules for collegial discussions, set specific goals and deadlines, and define individual roles as needed.

- CCSS.ELA-LITERACY.SL.8.5: Integrate multimedia and visual displays into presentations to clarify information, strengthen claims and evidence, and add interest.

- CCSS.ELA-LITERACY.W.8.1.B: Support claim(s) with logical reasoning and relevant evidence, using accurate, credible sources and demonstrating an understanding of the topic or text.

- CCSS.ELA-LITERACY.W.8.2.A: Introduce a topic clearly, previewing what is to follow; organize ideas, concepts, and information into broader categories; include formatting (e.g., headings), graphics (e.g., charts, tables), and multimedia when useful to aiding comprehension.

- CCSS.ELA-LITERACY.W.8.2.B: Develop the topic with relevant, well-chosen facts, definitions, concrete details, quotations, or other information and examples.

- CCSS.ELA-LITERACY.W.8.2.D: Use precise language and domain-specific vocabulary to inform about or explain the topic.

- CCSS.ELA-LITERACY.W.8.9: Draw evidence from literary or informational texts to support analysis, reflection, and research.

Common Core State Standards, English Language Arts, Literacy, History/Social Studies, Science and Technical Subjects (Grades 6-8) (Common Core State Standards Initiative, 2010)

- CCSS.ELA-LITERACY.RH.6-8.6: Identify aspects of a text that reveal an author's point of view or purpose (e.g., loaded language, inclusion or avoidance of particular facts).

- CCSS.ELA-LITERACY.RH.6-8.8: Distinguish among fact, opinion, and reasoned judgment in a text.

- CCSS.ELA-LITERACY.RST.6-8.8: Distinguish among facts, reasoned judgment based on research findings, and speculation in a text.

- CCSS.ELA-LITERACY.WHST.6-8.1.B: Support claim(s) with logical reasoning and relevant, accurate data and evidence that demonstrate an understanding of the topic or text, using credible sources.

- CCSS.ELA-LITERACY.WHST.6-8.2.A: Introduce a topic clearly, previewing what is to follow; organize ideas, concepts, and information into broader categories as appropriate to achieving purpose; include formatting (e.g., headings), graphics (e.g., charts, tables), and multimedia when useful to aiding comprehension.

- CCSS.ELA-LITERACY.WHST.6-8.2.B: Develop the topic with relevant, well-chosen facts, definitions, concrete details, quotations, or other information and examples.

- CCSS.ELA-LITERACY.WHST.6-8.9: Draw evidence from informational texts to support analysis, reflection, and research.

Next Generation Science Standards (Grades 6-8) (Next Generation Science Standards, undated)

- MS-ESS3-5 Earth and Human Activity: Ask questions to clarify evidence of the factors that have caused the rise in global temperatures over the past century[a]

[a] Specific to climate change brief and Q&A video.

Appendix C. Suggested Supports for Special Populations

In this appendix, we provide a few options—based on recognized sources—for providing supports for English learners, students with special education needs, and struggling learners. For more-comprehensive guidance and options for scaffolding instruction and making accommodations for special students, we recommend that educators consult such relevant sources as those listed in the footnote below or provided by their schools and/or districts.[1]

English Learners

To support English learners' (ELs) access to grade-level concepts and continued development of language skills, instruction needs to provide appropriate *language scaffolding*, which refers to providing supports for students' language development by tapping into their backgrounds and dominant languages or by providing students with multiple opportunities to engage with academic content at increasingly difficult levels of complexity. Educators can consider the following practices when scaffolding for ELs:

- Allow students to respond to questions orally instead of in writing. This creates opportunities for oral language development.

- Provide opportunities for students to work with or rehearse their responses with a peer before participating in class discussions. In our lessons, the use of think-pair-share (described in the text box with the same title in Lesson One) can aid in providing these opportunities.

- Identify and preview vocabulary with students. Our lesson plans and student printables identify and define key vocabulary, but teachers might wish to identify additional vocabulary terms that might be unfamiliar for their ELs.

- Draw on students' background knowledge. We have found that students' background knowledge of public policy is limited, but most have heard about the topics of climate change, immigration, COVID-19, and school start times and their impact on sleep. These are topics that are often in the news and/or that students may have personal connections with. The first lesson is meant to spark students' interest and engagement with these topics by activating their existing background knowledge. Specifically, the know–want to know–learn chart (described in the text box with the same title in Lesson One) explicitly asks students to consider what they already know and what they would like to learn about the public policy topic.

- Use reading strategies that support ELs, such as reading the text aloud, providing text segmentation to make the readings more digestible (e.g., use the jigsaw activity described in Lesson Two), check for comprehension by providing scaffolding questions, and/or require students to annotate text.

- Model tasks for students. Our lessons provide several prompts that ask teachers to model responses to several questions. In addition, completing tasks in pairs can provide ELs with access to peer modeling.

- Offer options for the assignments that students are asked to complete. For example, alternatives to writing responses might be verbal responses or hand-drawn images.

- Provide sentence frames for students with lower levels of language proficiency to scaffold their oral and/or written responses (e.g., In the videos, the researcher said that_____; I learned that public policy can include_____.).

---

[1] On English learners, see August, Fenner, and Snyder, 2014; August, McCardle, and Shanahan, 2014; Baker, Lesaux, et al., 2014; Deussen et al., 2008; EngageNY, 2014; EngageNY, 2015; English Learners Success Forum, undated; Goldenberg, 2013; Li, 2012; Neri et al., 2016; Piazza, Rao, and Protacio, 2015; Turkan, Bicknell, and Croft, 2012; WIDA, 2017. On students with special education needs and struggling learners, see Council for Exceptional Children, undated; Piazza, Rao, and Protacio, 2015.

- To support content understanding, consider creating teacher-completed graphic organizers to ensure that students can identify key concepts in a text or lesson. The printables in Appendix A already contain some tables to prompt students to identify key concepts, but teachers can add content to highlight other key concepts.

- Provide students with the option of participating in discussions or taking notes in their first language. For example, students can complete the student printable materials in their first language. This practice can support students in comprehending the subject matter and promote engagement in the activities.

Students with Special Education Needs or Struggling Learners

Students' special education needs vary considerably; therefore, a wide variety of supports and accommodations may be needed to support learning. In this section, we make suggestions to address the needs linked to general learning disabilities, which may also be helpful for struggling learners independent of their identification for special education services. The suggested practices for ELs may also be helpful for students with general learning disabilities and struggling learners. We encourage teachers to consult relevant sources and consider students' specific needs when deciding whether and how to implement any of the following suggested practices:

- Adjust the pacing of the activities. Our lesson plans are designed to take an estimated 45 minutes. However, some students may struggle to complete the activities in this time frame. Consider extending the time for particular tasks or the entire lesson, or segment the lesson plan into additional but shorter lessons. Specifically, students might need more time to complete the reading task in Lesson Two, the information-finding exercise in Lesson Three, and their videos/podcasts in Lesson Four.

- Provide additional and more-explicit instructions and details. For example, students might need more-explicit guidance on how to complete the know–want to know–learn chart (described in the text box with the same title in Lesson One).

- Use the think-pair-share strategy (described in the text box with the same title in Lesson One). All of our lesson plans provide opportunities for teachers to use this strategy, which can allow students more time to formulate and organize their thoughts and responses. The strategy can also help students participate in whole-class discussion.

- Segment larger texts or tasks into manageable chunks. In Lesson Two, we suggest that educators use a jigsaw strategy (see the text box with the same name) to segment the text into smaller sections, which can help struggling learners. In Lesson Four, teachers can revise the project instructions and segment the task into steps.

- Provide frequent formative feedback to make learning expectations clear for students and to provide specific guidance on how students' work can improve. Specifically, teachers can draw on students' responses to exit tickets to adapt their instruction by revisiting concepts and clarifying ideas in future lessons.

Abbreviations

AEP	American Educator Panels
CCSS	Common Core State Standards
CDC	Centers for Disease Control and Prevention
COVID-19	coronavirus disease 2019
EL	English learner
FRPL	free or reduced-price lunch
K-12	kindergarten through 12th grade
ML	media literacy
Q&A	question-and-answer

References

ABLConnect, "Research on Activity Types," Harvard University webpage, undated. As of May 12, 2020: https://ablconnect.harvard.edu/research

Aronson, E., C. Stephan, J. Sikes, N. Blaney, and M. Snapp, *The Jigsaw Classroom*, Beverly Hills, Calif.: Sage, 1978.

August, Diane, Diane Staehr Fenner, and Sydney Snyder, *Scaffolding Instruction for English Language Learners: A Resource Guide for English Language Arts*, Washington, D.C.: American Institutes for Research, 2014. As of March 25, 2022: https://www.engageny.org/resource/scaffolding-instruction-english-language-learners-resource-guides-english-language-arts-and/file/106261

August, Diane, Peggy McCardle, and Timothy Shanahan, "Developing Literacy in English Language Learners: Findings from a Review of the Experimental Research," *School Psychology Review*, Vol. 43, No. 4, December 2014, pp. 490–498.

Baker, Garrett, Susannah Faxon-Mills, Alice Huguet, John F. Pane, and Laura S. Hamilton, Approaches and Obstacles to Promoting Media Literacy Education in U.S. Schools, Santa Monica, Calif.: RAND Corporation, RR-A112-19, 2021. As of March 23, 2022: https://www.rand.org/pubs/research_reports/RRA112-19.html

Baker, Scott, Nonie Lesaux, Madhavi Jayanthi, Joseph Dimino, C. Patrick Proctor, Joan Morris, Russell Gersten, Kelly Haymond, Michael J. Kieffer, Sylvia Linan-Thompson, and Rebecca Newman-Gonchar, *Teaching Academic Content and Literacy to English Learners in Elementary and Middle School*, Washington, D.C.: U.S. Department of Education, Institute for Education Sciences, National Center for Education Evaluation and Regional Assistance, NCEE 2014-4012, April 2014.

Battelle for Kids, "P21 Partnership for 21st Century Learning: A Network of Battelle forKids," webpage, undated. As of March 30, 2022 http://www.battelleforkids.org/networks/p21

Beck, Laurie F., Jonathan Downs, Mark R. Stevens, and Erin K. Sauber-Schatz, "Rural and Urban Differences in Passenger-Vehicle–Occupant Deaths and Seat Belt Use Among Adults—United States, 2014," *Morbidity and Mortality Weekly Report*, Vol. 66, No. SS-17, 2017, pp. 1–13.

Breakstone, Joel, Mark Smith, Sam Wineburg, Amie Rapaport, Jill Carle, Marshall Garland, and Anna Saavedra, *Students' Civic Online Reasoning: A National Portrait*, Palo Alto, Calif.: Stanford History Education Group & Gibson Consulting, 2019.

Center for Media Literacy, "MediaLitKit: Five Key Questions of Media Literacy," handout, 2005. As of January, 2021: http://www.medialit.org/sites/default/files/14B_CCKQPoster+5essays.pdf

CDC—*See* Centers for Disease Control and Prevention.

Centers for Disease Control and Prevention, *WISQARS (Web-Based Injury Statistics Query and Reporting System),* Atlanta, Ga.: U.S. Department of Health and Human Services, database, 2015. As of September 2, 2020: https://www.cdc.gov/injury/wisqars/index.html

Centers for Disease Control and Prevention, "Seat Belts: Get the Facts," webpage, October 7, 2020. As of March 23, 2022: https://www.cdc.gov/transportationsafety/seatbelts/facts.html

Clemons, Trudy, Charles Igel, and Jessica Allen, "Cues, Questions, and Advance Organizers," in Andrea D. Beesley and Helen S. Apthorp, eds., *Classroom Instruction That Works,* 2nd ed., Denver, Col.: Mid-Continent Research for Education and Learning (McREL), 2010, pp. 130–139.

Common Core State Standards Initiative, *Common Core State Standards,* Washington, D.C.: National Governors Association Center for Best Practices & Council of Chief State School Officers, 2010. As of March 30, 2022: http://www.corestandards.org/wp-content/uploads/ELA_Standards1.pdf

Council for Exceptional Children, homepage, undated. As of March 25, 2022: https://www.cec.sped.org

Davis, Katie, "Shout Out: A Kid's Guide to Recording Stories," *Transom,* October 3, 2013.

Deussen, Theresa, Elizabeth Autio, Bruce Miller, Anne Turnbaugh Lockwood, and Victoria Stewart, *What Teachers Should Know About Instruction for English Language Learners: A Report to Washington State,* Portland, Ore.: Education Northwest, November 2008.

EngageNY, *Support for Students with Diverse Learning Needs, New York State Common Core ELA and Literacy Curriculum: Grade 9–12,* Albany, N.Y.: Public Consulting Group, February 2014.

EngageNY, *ELA Prefatory Material, New York State Common Core ELA and Literacy Curriculum: Grade 9–12,* Albany, N.Y.: Public Consulting Group, 2015. As of March 25, 2022: https://www.engageny.org/resource/prefatory-material-for-grades-9-12-english-language-arts

English Learners Success Forum, homepage, undated. As of March 25, 2022: https://www.elsuccessforum.org

Fowler, Kelsie, Mark Windschitl, and Jennifer Richards, "Exit Tickets," *The Science Teacher,* Vol. 86, No. 8, 2019, pp. 18–26.

Frayer, Dorothy Ann, Wayne C. Frederick, and Herbert J. Klausmeier, *A Schema for Testing the Level of Cognitive Mastery,* Madison, Wis.: Wisconsin Center for Education Research, 1969.

Garcia, Antero, Amber Maria Levinson, and Emma Carene Gargroetzi, "Dear Future President of the United States": Analyzing Youth Civic Writing Within the 2016 Letters to the Next President Project," *American Educational Research Journal,* Vol. 57, No. 3, 2020, pp. 1159–1202.

Ghaffar, May Abdul, Megan Khairallah, and Sara Salloum, "Co-Constructed Rubrics and Assessment for Learning: The Impact on Middle School Students' Attitudes and Writing Skills," *Assessing Writing,* Vol. 45, 2020.

Goldenberg, Claude, "Unlocking the Research on English Learners: What We Know—and Don't Yet Know—About Effective Instruction," *American Educator,* Vol. 37, No. 2, Summer 2013, pp. 4–38.

Guess, Andrew M., and Benjamin A. Lyons," Misinformation, Disinformation, and Online Propaganda," in Nathaniel Persily and Joshua A. Tucker, eds., *Social Media and Democracy: The State of the Field, Prospects for Reform,* Cambridge, United Kingdom: Cambridge University Press, 2020, pp. 10–33.

Hamilton, Laura S., Julia H. Kaufman, and Lynn Hu, *Media Use and Literacy in Schools: Civic Development in the Era of Truth Decay,* , Santa Monica, Calif.: RAND Corporation, RR-A112-2, 2020a. As of November 12, 2021: https://www.rand.org/pubs/research_reports/RRA112-6.html

Hamilton, Laura S., Julia H. Kaufman, and Lynn Hu, *Preparing Children and Youth for Civic Life in the Era of Truth Decay: Insights from the American Teacher Panel,* Santa Monica, Calif.: RAND Corporation, RR-A112-6, 2020b. As of November 12, 2021: https://www.rand.org/pubs/research_reports/RRA112-6.html

Hart, Daniel, Thomas M. Donnelly, James Youniss, and Robert Atkins, "High School Community Service as a Predictor of Adult Voting and Volunteering," *American Educational Research Journal,* Vol. 44, No. 1, 2007, pp. 197–219.

Hubbe, Alex, and Mark Hubbe, "Current Climate Change and the Future of Life on the Planet," *Frontiers for Young Minds,* March 7, 2019.

Huguet, Alice, Garrett Baker, Laura S. Hamilton, and John F. Pane, *Media Literacy Standards to Counter Truth Decay,* Santa Monica, Calif.: RAND Corporation, RR-A112-12, 2021. As of March 23, 2022: https://www.rand.org/pubs/research_reports/RRA112-12.html

Huguet, Alice, Jennifer Kavanagh, Garrett Baker, and Marjory S. Blumenthal, *Exploring Media Literacy Education as a Tool for Mitigating Truth Decay*, Santa Monica, Calif.: RAND Corporation, RR-3050-RC, 2019. As of March 23, 2022:
https://www.rand.org/pubs/research_reports/RR3050.html

Huguet, Alice, John F. Pane, Garrett Baker, Laura S. Hamilton, and Susannah Faxon-Mills, *Media Literacy Education to Counter Truth Decay: An Implementation and Evaluation Framework*, Santa Monica, Calif.: RAND Corporation, RR-A112-18, 2021. As of March 23, 2022:
https://www.rand.org/pubs/research_reports/RRA112-18.html

International Organization for Migration, *World Migration Report 2020*, interactive website, 2020. As of March 25, 2022:
https://worldmigrationreport.iom.int/wmr-2020-interactive/

Jolls, Tessa, and Michele Dorene Johnsen, "Media Literacy: A Foundational Skill for Democracy in the 21st Century," *Hastings Law Journal*, Vol. 69, No. 5, 2018, p. 1379.

Jolls, Tessa, and Carolyn Wilson, "The Core Concepts: Fundamental to Media Literacy Yesterday, Today and Tomorrow," *Journal of Media Literacy Education*, Vol. 6, No. 2, 2014, pp. 68–78.

Jonsson, Anders, and Gunilla Svingby, "The Use of Scoring Rubrics: Reliability, Validity, and Educational Consequences," *Educational Research Review*, Vol. 2, No. 2, 2007, pp. 130–144.

Kavanagh, Jennifer, and Michael D. Rich, *Truth Decay: An Initial Exploration of the Diminishing Role of Facts and Analysis in American Public Life*, Santa Monica, Calif.: R AND Corporation, RR-2314-RC, 2018. As of March 1, 2020:
https://www.rand.org/pubs/research_reports/RR2314.html

Kawashima-Ginsberg, Kei, and Peter Levine, "Policy Effects on Informed Political Engagement," *American Behavioral Scientist*, Vol. 58, No. 5, 2014, pp. 665–688.

KQED, "KQED Media Academy for Educators," webpage, undated. As of March 15, 2022:
https://teach.kqed.org/media-academy-for-educators

Learning Network, "Winners of Our Fourth Annual Podcast Contest," *New York Times*, July 1, 2021.

Leeder, Chris, "How College Students Evaluate and Share 'Fake News' Stories," *Library & Information Science Research*, Vol. 41, No. 3, 2019.

Levine, Peter, and Kei Kawashima-Ginsberg, *The Republic Is (Still) at Risk—and Civics Is Part of the Solution*, Medford, Mass.: Jonathan M. Tisch College of Civic Life, Tufts University, 2017.

Li, Jun, *Principles of Effective English Language Learner Pedagogy*, New York: College Board, 2012.

Lyman, Frank T., "The Responsive Classroom Discussion: The Inclusion of All Students," in Audrey Anderson, ed., *Mainstreaming Digest*, College Park, Md.: University of Maryland Press, 1981, pp. 109–113.

Martin, Florence, Chuang Wang, Teresa Petty, Weichao Wang, and P. Wilkins, "Middle School Students' Social Media Use," *Journal of Educational Technology & Society*, Vol. 21, No. 1, 2018, pp. 213–224.

National Highway Traffic Safety Administration, *Lives Saved in 2017 by Restraint Use and Minimum-Drinking-Age Laws*, Washington, D.C.: U.S. Department of Transportation, Publication no. DOT-HS-812-683, 2019. As of September 3, 2020:
https://crashstats.nhtsa.dot.gov/Api/Public/ViewPublication/812683

Neri, Rebecca, Maritza Lozano, Sandy Chang, and Joan Herman, *High-Leverage Principles of Effective Instruction for English Learners: From College and Career Ready Standards to Teaching and Learning in the Classroom: A Series of Resources for Teachers*, Los Angeles, Calif.: Center on Standards and Assessment Implementation, 2016.

Next Generation Science Standards, "MS-ESS3-5 Earth and Human Activity," webpage, undated. As of March 30, 2022:
https://www.nextgenscience.org/pe/ms-ess3-5-earth-and-human-activity

NPR, "Teaching Podcasting: A Curriculum Guide for Educators," webpage, November 15, 2018. As of March 30, 2022:
https://www.npr.org/2018/11/15/662116901/teaching-podcasting-a-curriculum-guide-for-educators

Ogle, Donna M., "The Know, Want to Know, Learn Strategy," in K. Denise Muth, ed., *Children's Comprehension of Text: Research into Practice*, Newark, Del.: International Literacy Association, 1989, pp. 205–223.

Piazza, Susan V., Shaila Rao, and Maria Selena Protacio, "Converging Recommendations for Culturally Responsive Literacy Practices: Students with Learning Disabilities, English Language Learners, and Socioculturally Diverse Learners," *International Journal of Multicultural Education*, Vol. 17, No. 3, 2015, pp. 1–20.

Slavin, Robert E., "Cooperative Learning in Elementary Schools," *Education 3-13*, Vol. 43, No. 1, 2015, pp. 5–14.

Stanford History Education Group, homepage, undated. As of March 23, 2022:
https://sheg.stanford.edu/

Tomlin, C. M., "Facts About Coronavirus: What Kids Need to Know," National Geographic Kids webpage, July 21, 2021. As of March 25, 2022:
https://kids.nationalgeographic.com/science/article/facts-about-coronavirus

Troxel, Wendy, "Teens Are Sleep Deprived; Later School Start Times Could Help," RAND Blog, March 4, 2020. As of March 23, 2022:
https://www.rand.org/blog/2020/03/teens-are-sleep-deprived-later-school-start-times.html

Tully, Melissa, and Emily K. Vraga, "Who Experiences Growth in News Media Literacy and Why Does It Matter? Examining Education, Individual Differences, and Democratic Outcomes," *Journalism & Mass Communication Educator*, Vol. 73, No, 2, 2018, pp. 167–181.

Turkan, Sultan, Jerome Bicknell, and Andrew Croft, *Effective Practices for Developing the Literacy Skills of English Language Learners in the English Language Arts Classroom*, Princeton, N.J.: ETS, ETS Research Report Series, RR-12-03, 2012, pp. i–31.

University of Minnesota Libraries, "Profiles in Teaching and Learning with Student Media Projects," webpage, 2021. As of March 1, 2022:
https://libguides.umn.edu/c.php?g=1138002

Webb, Theresa, and Kathryn Martin, "Evaluation of a US School-Based Media Literacy Violence Prevention Curriculum on Changes in Knowledge and Critical Thinking Among Adolescents," *Journal of Children and Media*, Vol. 6, No. 4, 2012, pp. 430–449.

WIDA, *2012 Amplification of the English Language Development Standards: Kindergarten–Grade 12*, Madison, Wisc.: Board of Regents of the University of Wisconsin System, February 6, 2017. As of March 25, 2022:
https://wida.wisc.edu/sites/default/files/resource/2012-ELD-Standards.pdf

Yoder, Nick, and Deb Gurke, *Social and Emotional Learning Coaching Toolkit: Keeping SEL at the Center*, Washington, D.C.: American Institutes for Research, August 2017.

Zywica, Jolene, and Kimberly Gomez, "Annotating to Support Learning in the Content Areas: Teaching and Learning Science," *Journal of Adolescent & Adult Literacy*, Vol. 52, No. 2, 2008, pp. 155–165.